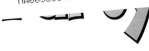

MW00566040

by Pepe Ramirez
illustrated by John Berg

 HOUGHTON MIFFLIN   BOSTON

Printed in China

ISBN 10: 0-618-88595-1
ISBN 13: 978-0-618-88595-4

456789 0940 16 15 14 13 12 11
4500334673

"Let's have a garden party,"
said Katy.
"Oh, yes," agreed Milly. "We'll all
go to Mr. Green's garden."

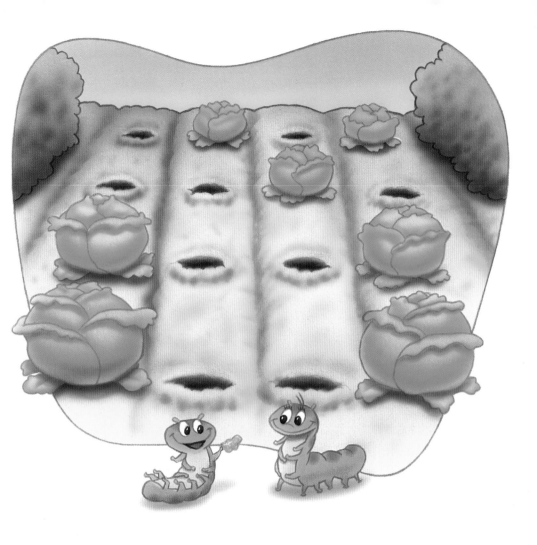

Mr. Green has 16 lettuce plants.

"It's delicious!" said Mikey.

They ate 9 lettuce plants.

How many lettuce plants are left?

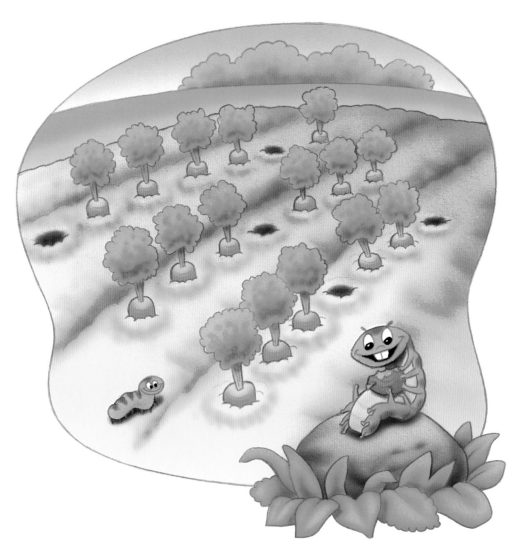

Mr. Green has 21 carrots.
"Yummy!" said Danny.
They ate 5 carrots. Mmm!

How many carrots are left?

Mr. Green has 30 pepper plants.

"My favorite!" said Greta.

They ate 9 peppers.

How many peppers are left?

Mr. Green has 18 beets.

"Tasty!" said Tina.

They ate 18 beets.

How many beets are left?

"Oh, oh," said Skippy. "I hear
Mr. Green coming."
And so, they all began to crawl.
Humpity bump.
Humpity bump.

How many caterpillars stayed in the garden?

The Caterpillars' Feast

Draw

Look at page 3. Draw the lettuce garden you see. Draw an X for each head of lettuce that is gone.

Tell About

Look at page 3. Tell how many heads of lettuce Mr. Green planted. Tell how many heads of lettuce the caterpillars ate.

Write

Solve Problems/Make Decisions **Look at page 3. Write how many heads of lettuce are left in the garden.**